The Good Shepherd's Heart

—— LIVING PARABLES ——

Tracy Hogan

MANIFEST
PUBLICATIONS

The Good Shepherd's Heart: Living Parables
Copyright © 2019 Tracy Hogan
ALL RIGHTS RESERVED WORLDWIDE
Manifest International, LLC

ISBN: 978-1-951280-04-8

Unless otherwise noted, scripture quotations are taken from the New King James Version (NKJV). Copyright © 1982 by Thomas Nelson, Inc. Used by permission. All rights reserved.

The Amplified Bible. Copyright © 1954, 1958, 1962, 1964, 1965, 1987 by the Lockman Foundation. Used by permission. All rights reserved.

New International Version (NIV). Holy Bible, New International Version, NIV Copyright ©1973, 1978, 1984, 2011 by Biblica, Inc. Used by permission. All rights reserved.

Scriptures noted "AP" are the author's own paraphrase.

Cover Design: Chelsea Mckeown, The Voice of My Beloved.
Typesetting: The Voice of My Beloved.

Dedication

Father in Heaven, forever thank you for choosing me, the most unlikely, to be entrusted with this holy work. Thank you for Your patient, kind love that never fails me.

Lamb of God – Yeshua our Eternal King, forever thank you for the journey – for all that You are teaching me. For entrusting me to share Your ever so noble, beautiful heart with Your beloved ones – the ones Whom You died for so that we can be restored to Your eternal plans – to be Your Bride.

You are the Good Shepherd. Who alone is my Beautiful Savior, my Majestic Reigning Conquering King, my ever so Just, Righteous Lord and Law Giver. Who is my Strategic Master Builder, the Captain of my salvation – my healer, deliverer, rescuer, redeemer, restorer – Who provides my every need.

You are my nearest and dearest, kindest and bestest friend – my constant companion. The Lover of my soul, my faithful Bridegroom King, my Song of Solomon – my fearless and fearsome hero. You are the only One whom my soul loveth and adores. Lord Yeshua, You alone reign and You alone are worthy.

May You, my Beloved King, be magnified in these writings, drawing Your Bride, even closer yet into Your heart, all for Your glory, forever and ever! Amen!

Acknowledgements

With a heart overflowing with eternal gratitude, I want to thank my beloved, and dearly treasured ministry partners, Chelsea Mckeown and Christine Culhane for their endless, faithful sacrificial love and prayers enabling this book to come forth.

Chelsea, you have been my Timothy and Barnabas – could not imagine this journey without you. Forever thank you for all the ways that you have labored – your time, energy, resources, the giftings and anointings that our Father in heaven has blessed you with, sharing every step of the Good Shepherd's heart with me – enabling this book to come into completion. You are my beautiful, beloved, dearest daughter that I love and cherish! This world is a much better place because our Father in heaven created you for such a time as this!

Christine, what words could ever say thank you enough for all the ways you have sacrificed in every way possible, over and over again! You have been my hands and feet in more ways than I could ever keep track of, enabling me to be free to do the work of our Father's hands. You are a faithful and true friend, anointed and committed prayer partner, a sister, and a dearly beloved daughter that I love and adore!

Lastly, mom, forever thank you for your sacrificial, endless love and encouragement! For all your prayers of a 'mom' that are like no others that are prayed on my behalf before His throne of grace. And especially for all those prayers during the night hours, when you thought no one noticed, or they were not being heard. They have not only been heard, but felt and answered! You are not only the best mom I could hope to have, but you are a true intercessor – this book would not have happened without your love and prayers. I love you!

Foreword

I have never met anyone like Tracy. Of course, that is an understatement. Our Father has made all of us wonderfully different. But how we add to that makes all the difference in the world. I have always known her to be a woman who loves the Lord, and that love is constantly growing. I had noticed her ability to look deeply into words and allow them to reverberate fruitfully from her lips. It was then that I asked her to edit my book, *Suffering Unto Perfection* – to God be the glory.

Now after many years, and writing her own book, you will enjoy the journey she takes you on with our Lord. Gracefully causing you to gaze into His heart and see His great love, not only for you but for all of humanity. Causing you to fall in love more and more with the King.

DR. EUGENE UNDERWOOD
Spirit Life Ministries,
Special Forces School of Ministries
Anchorage, AK, USA

Endorsements

The Good Shepherd's Heart is a deep and wondrous journey into the meditations of a hidden prophetic intercessor, majestically set in the rolling hills and pasturelands of the western Irish seacoast. This unique collection of real-life parables gives us a tangible revelation of the Lord's nature – that of the Good Shepherd of His flock.

Tracy takes us along her prayer walks, narrating her encounters and dramatic rescue missions, as she is led to observe, comfort, and intervene for various lost, trapped or injured lambs. With each parable, she also includes vital biblical teachings that connect her life-saving interventions (and the lambs' responses to her offers of help), with the principles of obedience, trust, and discipleship in our own walks with the Lord. In each encounter, the Lord demonstrates another aspect of His love, concern, and at times, His necessary discipline for His people's wounded, trapped, lost, or endangered spiritual conditions.

Tracy's heart to help and direct these sheep or lambs to safety reflects the fierce and tender emotions of the Lord for each of us. She also shares the glory of the Lord's Presence, affection, and the panoramic splendor of His creation, as He strongly manifests His heart and His beauty to her in this idyllic pastoral backdrop.

As Tracy opens to us her intimate journal of a loving shepherd's motives and strategies of rescue, we see our own lack of trust in the Lord's good intentions to help us, not to harm us. We see how aptly Isaiah described us as sheep who had gone astray, and who needed a rescuing Shepherd to show us the way home.

May this amazing jewel collection of living parables cause us to trust the Lord more – even if He has to wound us before He can heal us. We are His people and the flock of His hand. May your heart be enlarged and enriched by this powerful and intensely intimate revelation of the Shepherd's Loving Heart.

JILL SHANNON
Author, Songwriter

Feel the always tender, sometimes tense, pulse of love sought, love lost, love found, love touched, love sensed, love graced, love offered, love received in these memorable vignettes of an illustrious handmaiden of heaven as she takes her bucolic walks with the Shepherd and Lover of her soul. Tracy Hogan is a friend who loves, like the Bible tells, at all times and a sister born for adversity. Witness the courage, learn the disciplines, share the joys of a true daughter of Zion within these godly pages!

PASTOR BERNARD LEE
Jesus Endtimes Ministries,
Richmond BC, Canada

I have known Tracy for the last few years and have come to know her as a woman of integrity and holds the anointing of a true intercessor. This generation must go beyond the norm through intercession and relationship with our Lord.

The life of Tracy in this book is an inspiration that all of us need to walk according to the leading of the Holy Spirit. The end result being that we all become overcomers.

What a blessing to know that we are joined together for the work of the Lord. I hope all who read this book get encouraged.

PASTOR JOSE ROCO
Mahanaim Life Ministry
Sydney, Australia

Since I have gotten to know Tracy Hogan, I see she is totally sold-out to live for her beloved Bridegroom and soon coming King – Jesus Christ. Her relationship with Him is real and deep, and this book is written from that reality. She consistently brings out the importance of having an intimate relationship with our Good Shepherd – Jesus, Lover of our soul.

MARY O'SULLIVAN
Lydia Fellowship County Leader,
Prophetic Intercessor,
Beaufort, County Kerry, Ireland

I gladly recommend this book, *The Good Shepherd's Heart: Living Parables* by my good friend, Tracy Hogan. We all need to grow continually in first love, especially by realising how much Jesus, The Good Shepherd, truly loves us all, irrespective of our background or denomination. His love is deep, heartfelt but above all, unforced. True love is never forced.

The ten parables in this book illustrate the above-mentioned points very clearly. They are true stories about straying or trapped sheep and lambs. Each story is very unique and differs in detail from all the others. They are also very riveting, insofar as the final outcome is not at all obvious, and the reader's curiosity is sustained to the end.

The variety and diversity is remarkable and appropriately portray the rich diversity in human nature. Above all, they bring out our needless fear of the Shepherd, our blindness to His perfect love, and our blindness to the potentially fatal hazards of straying from Him.

Each story is followed by a biblical reflection on the character of Jesus. He is so compassionate and patient. He truly grieves at our lack of awareness of His love. He is continually calling us but never intrudes on our freedom. I encourage you to read and be blessed.

PASCHAL COFFEY
Ballincollig, County Cork, Ireland

These parables, that are so well written and inspirational, took me to a new place of revelation into the nature of God. I was wonderfully inspired by the words so expertly penned, then motivated to seek the Lord on a deeper level of intimacy, as this faithful servant has so graciously exampled in this book.

As I journeyed through each encounter, I was reminded of the first commandment, to love the Lord your God with your whole heart, mind, soul, and strength. Such a complete commitment – a call to be all consumed in total surrender, to a relationship with the Father. These parables show the relationship God desires to have with everyone – a relationship that involves our every waking hour. A relationship with the Good Shepherd that teaches us how all healthy relationships grow and are sustained.

They further show how God in all His majesty and complexity can reach down into our daily lives, to even the most primal experience and make them truly miraculous. Tracy has expertly portrayed the majesty and simplicity of Yeshua's parables while capturing the wonder of His complex presence. For Tracy, it is being with the sheep and the mysteries of the Kingdom revealed through these encounters. For me, the stories remain to be written.

Thank you for these beautiful parables. Your faithful obedience to the Father will, I'm sure, bless many into His loving presence, while encouraging us to live in that spiritual relationship with Him as He perfects in us the image of Yeshua. Too often messages tell us what to do but not how. Because of your obedience to God and your love in sharing the experience with us, we can realize the 'how,' as He reflects His image through you. This book is now a cherished addition to my library.

RICK LANCE
Palmdale, CA, USA

Contents

	Introduction	1
1	Rescue, Heal And Restore	3
2	The Wilderness – A Journey Of Intimacy	9
3	Yours Is The Kingdom – Nothing Can Stand Against It	15
4	There Is No Fear In Love	20
5	He Gently Leads Those That Have Young	24
6	Keep Asking, Keep Seeking – Keep Knocking	31
7	His Ways Are Not Our Ways	36
8	His Patience Wins Many	41
9	Blinded By Pain	50
10	Resurrection Life	56

Introduction

These parables are an account of my real-life encounters with the Good Shepherd, which are by His divine design, and contain the heavenly jewels of revelation, wisdom and priceless lessons in leadership and stewardship that He has graciously taught me. These encounters began soon after arriving in Ireland in late September 2015. They take place on the countless prayer walks we have done, walking the beautiful farmland and coastal shores in County Kerry. They are what I call Living Parables where the Master Teacher has me walk something out in the natural, then makes me very aware He is there to teach me a spiritual lesson, wanting me to see another facet of His beautiful Good Shepherd's heart.

After about eight or nine months, I started to understand what the Good Shepherd was doing. He was showing me how priceless and beautiful the sheep are to Him. Helping me see and understand the sheep from His heart, and the great lengths that He goes to in order to restore them back to His sheepfold where they belong. As too often they are left wandering outside their sheepfolds; confused, frightened, injured, covered in filth, bleeding, lame, and some left for dead, with no one to help them.

Often during these times, I would cry out, *"Lord, where are the shepherds, why are they not here checking on their flock and taking care of them, doesn't this upset You Lord?"* I would be so distressed to see these precious sheep left without help, and before I knew it, we were on a rescue mission, as I could not leave a lamb or sheep without getting it the help it needed, or restored back to its sheepfold. I learned a lot about sheep!

It was in these rescue missions the Lord would speak to me about His church – the sheep and the pastors, and how often, at large, His sheep are neglected with few good shepherds tending to His flock the way He expects them to. And, at the same time, how stubborn or foolish the sheep can be when Godly counsel comes their way. That so often they reject it, choosing to go their own way.

Therefore, making it difficult to lead them in the way they are to go.

In these encounters, the Lord was causing me to be utterly broken for His 'sheep' in Ireland, by using the sheep of the land to break my heart to millions of pieces. This in itself was an answer to the prayer I had prayed so often soon after arriving, *"Lord give me Your burden for Ireland, break my heart the way Yours breaks for this Nation. Give me Your tears for this Nation."*

When you are called to intercede for a nation, you have to be broken for it. It is that brokenness that enables you to carry the burden He has given you. The Good Shepherd surely accomplished that in those first eight to nine months after my arrival, and is faithful to keep me in that place of being broken not only for this Nation, but equally for His church and Israel.

With that introduction, it is my humblest honor to be able to share the Good Shepherd's heart with you. I pray that these accountings will bless you, strengthen you, and encourage you as you run to finish the race that is set before you. May you hear the Good Shepherd's voice calling you closer to His bosom – deeper into His heart. Calling you into the eternal plans He has for you – to be the Bride of Messiah!

Chapter 1

Rescue, Heal And Restore

Weeks before this encounter took place, the Lord had been speaking to me about brokenness. How we have a lot of broken Christians who keep breaking people, instead of bringing healing to others. How so few are truly broken before Him with their hearts breaking for what His heart breaks for. That until we mature in Him, we will keep breaking people, instead of being broken for them to be healed.

May you hear the Good Shepherd's voice calling you closer to His bosom – calling you to that place of brokenness so He can heal and restore you to your full inheritance in Him!

After finishing our prayer call around 6:00 A.M. I continued to pray in the spirit until about 7:20 A.M. finishing my time of prayer at 7:50 A.M. As I finished, I asked *"Lord can we go for a prayer walk and just keep praying, pray for Ireland, pray for this ministry to do what You are asking of us? Would You please come with me Lord, You know I don't ever want to go anywhere without You. Please come – teach me how to pray."*

That is my normal custom, I always ask the Lord to come with me and to teach me how to pray. Often during these times, I just pray in the spirit. Since I get up very early for our prayer call, I normally would not go for a walk on Tuesdays, due to fatigue, as I still needed to prepare for our 3:00 P.M. prayer watch. But this morning I felt refreshed, so we headed out the door soon after 8:00 A.M. In the first few minutes I was aware that I was feeling really good, and thanking the Lord for He had surely given me a grace that I don't normally feel, after so little sleep!

I had planned to do our shortest walk, which is about four miles, taking me up and down hills, through quiet farmland. About halfway, on the windy back roads where there are flocks of sheep with their new lambs; I noticed two lambs near the wire fence. They were away from their mom and the rest of their flock, investigating their surroundings.

I smiled at how adorable they were, but at the same time I was concerned for their safety, so I gently scolded them as I walked by, and told them they needed to get back to their flock and not wander – they need to stick together! Within seconds they turned and ran back to their flock! I stopped to watch them smiling at their innocence, yet concerned for how unaware they are of potential dangers.

At the same time, I could hear baaing ahead. By the sound, I knew it was a lamb. After a few more yards I could discern it was a lamb in trouble, but I could not see it. I also heard what I assumed was its' mom baaing. I stopped in front of a gate listening a few more seconds saying, *"Lord, that is clearly a lamb in trouble – we have to go help it!"*

So, we climbed over the metal gate, into mucky mud, down the hill, past a wooded, wet marshy area following the sound of the baaing. I still could not see the lamb at this point. But after a few more yards I could see it was on the other side of a broken down stonewall, near a ditch next to the wire fencing that separated this flock from the one in the field across from where it was.

As I got closer, and to my horror, I could now see just how in trouble this precious, beautiful, little lamb was. To make it worse, she became frightened by me and was trying to frantically pull herself free from the wire fence that had become a trap for her. I kept reassuring her that there was no need to be afraid.

She had somehow managed to get her left hind hoof entangled in the wire fencing, so it had twisted around her shank bone like a rubber band. She was literally hanging in mid-air with her head towards the ditch and her front hooves barely able to touch the ground! I feared she had pulled her hip out of its socket! It was a terrible sight!

As I approached her, she started pulling even more, which was so painful to watch. I quickly grabbed her by the back of the neck and pulled her up so her head was level to stop her struggling, until I could figure out how to free her. I kept reassuring her that I was there to help her. Within seconds she became calm and quiet.

I asked the Lord, *"How do we get her free Lord, how? Please show me."* I then picked her up, cradling her with my arms, so she was tightly next to my chest, taking the pressure off her hind legs completely, enabling me to unwrap the wire from around her shank. She was free in seconds – Praise the Lord! But I knew she was badly injured – not knowing how many hours she had been dangling from this fence over the ditch! It was also not straightforward getting back to the flock that was in the field above, which is where I was pretty sure she belonged too, but I was not certain.

So, there was no way I was letting go of her until I knew which flock to return her too. And if it was the field above where she belonged, then I would have to carry her a certain distance to get her there. As I held her tightly against my chest, with her head snuggled near my left shoulder, I quickly evaluated the flock across from me and the one above, and at the same time looking at the fence, and how I found her, I was pretty certain she belonged to the flock above.

Once that was determined, I just held her in that place of brokenness and spoke healing and restoration in her and over her, praying, *"Lord heal her, heal and restore – restore her in every way she needs it emotionally from the trauma and especially physically in her hip and leg."*

I did not know yet how badly she was injured as I had held her the whole time. But I could not help but think of how a 'good shepherd' teaches his lambs to depend on him by breaking one of their legs, and then holding them so close to his bosom until they are healed.

As I was thinking of that, how he has to discipline those that go astray in order to keep them safe in their fold where they belong, I was holding this little girl that was beautiful beyond description so close to my bosom. I was in awe to find myself in this position, so in awe of the Good Shepherd! My heart was melting to a million pieces! I would stroke her head, giving her soft kisses. She was so peaceful, so beautiful! There was nothing in me that wanted to let go – I wanted to hold her forever!

I was cherishing these priceless moments, as I was very aware the Good Shepherd was there wanting me to have this intimate encounter with Him. I was so humbled He would allow me to be so close to that which He holds so tightly, trusting me with this priceless lamb, to rescue her, to pray for her healing and restoration. I kept thanking Him for this priceless time that I did not want to end.

But time could delay no more, and after several minutes, I carried the lamb out of the marshy mire, over the broken-down wall and set her on the ground to see how badly she was injured. She immediately leapt off on three legs, running and baaing to the comfort and familiarity of her mom and sibling. I was happy to see them united, but my heart hurt that her hip was badly injured and kept asking the Lord to bring total restoration to her.

I slowly made my way back across the field, keeping my eye on her, watching as mom, sibling, and herself walked to a quiet place in the field away from the rest of the flock. At times I would just stop and watch – it was hard to leave her.

Several times she would stop and look back at me. At one point, she looked back and we just stared at each other, her gaze meeting mine – my heart desperately wanting her to be healed. It was in that moment I spoke to her and said, *"The Lord rescues us to heal us, and if we are not broken, He cannot restore."*

As soon as I spoke those words, I knew it was the Lord speaking through me and He stopped me in my tracks – this is what He wanted me to understand on a Kingdom level. It is something He had already been speaking to me about in the past few weeks, especially as we pray for the broken-down walls and ruins of His remnant to be rebuilt and restored to truth, so we can rebuild the broken-down walls of our Nation.

A word He had given me the night before was, "*I can only restore that which is broken.*" Referring to His people and how we need to come to a place of complete brokenness before Him, so that He can heal and restore us back to the fullness of our rightful inheritance in Him. Without that brokenness and becoming completely dependent upon Him to heal and transform us His way, it is not possible to restore us to that place of intimate fellowship, as He longs to have with us – to be His Bride.

He was further showing me in this parable, that it is the Good Shepherd Who leads us to our places of being broken. Why? So He can heal and restore us, if we will trust Him, and let Him do it His way. It is in that place of intimate relationship that we learn to no longer be fearful trying to escape His ways, but instead we learn to trust Him in our afflictions, embracing them so He can work them for our good.

That just like that little lamb, although injured and on three legs, she was able to run and find her way back to her mom – to the security of her sheepfold where she belonged – to the place of her healing and transformation. So too, our breakings will cause us to hear the Good Shepherd's voice, leading us back to His bosom.

His heart is to bring restoration to our brokenness, but it can only come if we no longer run from Him. Sometimes in His amazing love for us, He sets what I call 'liquid love traps' where He will hem us in every way possible that the only escape will be into His loving embrace. He desires us far more than we do Him, and cares for our safety and well-being more than we ever could ourselves. So, He allows situations in our lives, helping us to return to Him wholeheartedly.

Our breakings can be very painful to our hearts and emotions, but He is a good Father, Who knows it will be for our good. As painful as it is for Him to watch His children suffer, He knows it will mean the broken fellowship between Him and us will be restored.

I overwhelmingly felt the Good Shepherds' heart in a greater measure of how beautiful and priceless we are to Him. For how great is His love for us! What great lengths He will go to in order to rescue, heal and restore us. And in our brokenness, we can be assured He will hold us ever so tight to His bosom, bringing the healing and restoration that only He can provide.

His heart never lets go of us. Instead, all too often, we are the ones that run from Him, fighting to be free from His loving embrace because the breakings in our lives hurt too much. We do not think we can stand the pain. But the truth is, if we fight to be free from Him in our breakings, we will end up hurting ourselves more, crippled in our walk with Him, limping along not ever able to receive all that He has for us.

But, if we are like that precious lamb and can receive the help that comes our way, as frightening and unfamiliar as it may seem to us at the time, He will enable us to leap forth in our brokenness. Giving us what we need to follow Him wherever He may lead, despite our injuries, so that He can heal and restore us in the fullest measure.

Sometimes though, the Lord has to let us go so we can learn by our mistakes. So we can learn to trust Him to bring us through the marshy, mire pits that we can find ourselves in, that only He can carry us out of.

It is in those times that we experience and learn to trust in the goodness of God, causing us to become more dependent upon Him – when we realize just how incapable we are to rescue ourselves. And, not only how capable the Good Shepherd is to rescue us, but how willing He is to rescue, heal and restore, if we let Him do it His way!

Come, and let us return to the Lord; for He has torn, but He can heal us; He has stricken, but He will bind us up. For how great is Your goodness and how great is Your beauty Lord [Hosea 6:1, Zechariah 9:17, AP]. AMEN!

Chapter 2

The Wilderness – A Journey Of Intimacy

Do you feel like you have been in the wilderness for years with no end in sight? It is a dry, barren place that all too often is confusing and painful, so we run trying to find our way out! If we do though, we will miss the Good Shepherd's plans for us, and why He brings us into the wilderness – so that we can find the Lover of our soul.

May you hear the Good Shepherd's voice calling you closer to His bosom – calling you to lean on His strength and never-failing love, as He carries you over the mountain tops, into the valleys below, into a deeper place of intimacy, in your wilderness experience.

This morning after waking and coming before the Lord for my time of prayer, I was a bit restless – really wanting to go for a prayer walk as it did not work out for me to do so for the past couple of days. After conversing with the Lord for about a half-hour, I asked, *"Lord, can we just go for a walk and pray?"* Soon after that, we headed out the door and my heart was so happy!

It was a beautiful, sunny, summer day and there was still a coolness in the morning air that I was enjoying, as the weather forecast was to be another hot day – unseasonable hot! As I enjoyed His beautiful creation that was all around me, I was contemplating which way to go. I decided on one of our longer walks that we had not done in some time.

With that settled, I was soon in that comfortable place that is all too familiar to me in my times with the Lord. That place where there is no pushing or pulling, but instead where the rhythm of my feet are in unison with His footsteps, where the Captain of my salvation leads, causing my heart to beat to the rhythm of my Beloved's.

As we walked the windy roads, up the hills to a high place that becomes open land that is surrounded by craggy mountains, there was nothing out of the ordinary in our journey. A few ewes were running ahead of me. This would be typical for this particular area as some of the land has no fencing and the sheep roam at will. There were a few sheep and lambs to either side of me, who decided to stay off the road!

I continued walking down a steep hill, passing fenced fields on my left and right. As I did, I was aware of baaing in the distance, behind me. I did not pay too much attention to it other than being aware of it, as I did not see the ewe or lamb. I kept praying and when I made it to the forest area, I took a short break and then headed back the way I came. Rarely do I go back the same way that I come, but today that was the plan.

While making my way back up the steep hill, I became increasingly aware of that one ewe's baaing, discerning by her voice she was in distress. Near the top of the hill, I stopped and searched intently with my eyes, quickly scanning the open land – the base of the mountains and the lower valley, trying to find her – asking, *"Where is she Lord?"*

Everywhere I looked I just saw open land – no ewes or lambs, but I kept hearing her pitiable baa! I looked one more time, in the direction of her voice, and I saw her! She was now standing on a high, craggy hill all by herself and let out one more pitiable baa.

As she stood there, I was trying to understand what was perplexing her. From what I could see she was alone, as I had once again looked at the open land that we had just passed, and the mountain behind her, not seeing any other sheep. This precious ewe was not injured, but she was clearly distressed – trying to find her flock – the one she belongs to. As she stood on that high hill, and from where I was standing, I spoke tender mercies to her, trying to comfort her in her distress.

In that moment, her eyes met mine, and with renewed determination, she headed down that high, craggy hill, heading straight towards me! I was pleasantly surprised as my heart hurt for her, and if I could somehow encourage or comfort her in that place of loneliness, fear, confusion, feeling lost or abandoned that she was experiencing, I would with great joy.

I kept speaking loving encouragement to her as she made her way down, reassuring her this is somehow going to be ok. As soon as I said this, and right before she got to me, I looked to my right – to the valley below, and I now saw two other ewes nestled against a large boulder. They were not there moments before for I had earnestly searched the land, scanning it for her flock finding none. I was overjoyed to see them!

Although they were a distance away, they were in the same fenced land. If this ewe, who was now in front of me, would take the right steps, find the right path through the tall grass that could block her vision, she would be reunited with them.

As soon as I had these thoughts, she made a sharp left taking her down the hill, through the high grass, headed towards the valley below, that would bring her to the ones' whom she belonged to.

At this point, there was no way I could leave, nor did I have a desire to do so, until I knew she had made it. Even though it seemed certain she had found the way that would bring her out of her wilderness journey, I had to see with my own eyes that she made it. So, I stood there watching her every step. My heart was happy for her, and I continued to shout out encouragement from afar saying, *"You're going to make it, how beautiful she was and how proud I was of her for climbing over the craggy, mountain and hills and into the valley below, and that she was going to make it."*

I was feeling how much Yeshua loved her not wanting her to feel so distressed and fearful, despite her uncomfortable situation.

She was almost there, with one small hill separating her from her flock. Her option was to either go left or right. If left, that would bring her to her flock. If right, it would take her around the hill and away from them from what I could see from afar. So, I quickly shouted out, *"Left, left, precious you need to go left!"* But she went right!

My heart became anxious for I feared she had made the wrong choice. But I was soon relieved when I saw that her choice did not cause her to miss her flock. For whatever reasons as to why she chose to go what 'seemed' a longer way, what mattered is she made it – Praise the Lord!

Although I was a distance away, watching from afar, I felt the peace that had been restored to all of us. But most all the peace that had been restored to that precious ewe that had found herself, on a lonely, wilderness journey, on a very hot day – parched, hot, her emotions wearied, yet with patient endurance, determined to find the ones' she belonged to.

So, too our Good Shepherd watches over our every step, with such tender, loving-kindness and mercies, not wanting us to feel distressed, fearful and anxious when we find ourselves in our own wilderness journey – the trials and afflictions that come our way. The wilderness is not a pleasant place – it is often painful, lonely, confusing and full of disappointments, heartache, rejection, fear and what seems like failures, or going the wrong way.

But it is a necessary place in our Christian walk if we are to grow and mature into bridal love – to be the Bride of Messiah. It is a place where the Refiner's fire comes, increasing the heat through situations in our lives with the purpose to draw out the dross in our souls – the imperfections in our character, so not only to deliver us from self, but ultimately to restore us back to His bosom. Back to that place of intimacy with the Lover of our soul.

Make no mistake beloved, it is our Bridegroom King Yeshua's relentless, fiery jealous love that woos and draws us into the wilderness. Where often just like that lone ewe, standing on a craggy, high hill, we find ourselves standing all alone – feeling lost, confused, weary in our emotions and bodies, suffering much loss emotionally and physically, not sure how to go on, or which way to turn.

He does so not because He is cruel or angry with us. No! In fact, it is the exact opposite. He longs for us to be one with Him – to be His

Bride, the one He died for, to be by His side for all of eternity. He will only marry a bride who has an undivided heart, no other lovers but Him.

So He uses our wilderness experiences to prove our hearts, letting us decide if we want to deny ourselves, take up our cross and follow Him, wherever He may lead. Or, will we turn to someone else or something else to satisfy our fleshly desires?

Our Bridegroom King is a gentleman Who will not force Himself upon us. So in His goodness and faithfulness towards us, He allows situations in our lives to help us let go of those things stopping us from following Him wholeheartedly. It is in the wilderness that if we follow Him wholeheartedly, we will find the Lover of our soul, developing an intimate love relationship with Him. For it is in that place that we learn to lean upon Him to meet our every need. Discovering He not only desires to meet our needs but takes care of us in every way possible, like no other!

So, beloved if you are finding yourself in the wilderness, going through painful, difficult times, know our Good Shepherd has not abandoned nor forsaken you, even though it can feel like it. Know instead He is calling you to a deeper place of intimacy, into a love relationship where you trust Him 100% to provide your every need.

If you will keep trusting and calling out for the One you love to help you, and no longer depend on yourself or man to do so, be assured His faithfulness will lead you in the way you are to go. It does not mean it will get easier – as often it gets harder. Just like the ewe, once she climbed the craggy, high hill where she could finally see hope again, she then descended to the valley below for it was the only way for her to find the one she belonged to.

So too, we will walk through the valleys that are the hardest part of our journey. When in the valley it is hard to see your way out for it all looks the same. It can feel like a really dry, barren, parched place to be. But if we let the Good Shepherd lead and we don't go by what we see or feel, especially when it 'seems' we are headed the wrong way, we can be assured He has not for a moment taken His eyes off us. He will be faithful to watch over every step we take, encouraging us along the way. He will keep us on the narrow path that leads to life, restoring us to the One our souls adore, in fullness.

One mistake we often make, when we find ourselves in the wilderness, is that we try to find a quick way out. We do so because the fire is hotter than we think we can bear – too painful, feeling like it will never end! Instead of trying to save ourselves, it is better to surrender our will right then and there to the Good Shepherd, letting Him lead us where we need to go, for however long He determines and not try to take a short cut.

He sees our end. He alone knows what we are called to suffer through that will bring us to the end result of our faith, to be His Bride. If we do it His way, the journey will purify our soul, molding and shaping us into His character, qualifying us to be His Bride. It will look different for each of us. And just like that ewe, it 'looked' like she was to go one way, but she went what I thought was the wrong way, because it was longer and I could not see where that path would take her. In the end, she reached her goal – restored to the ones' whom she belonged to.

Beloved, the Good Shepherd cares more about our holiness and obedience than what is convenient for us. Therefore, it is in our patient, endurance, as we learn to embrace the cross, overcoming trials and afflictions His way, walking through the wilderness clinging to the One we love, where we are restored to that place of intimacy that He longs to have with us. And in that place, despite what is happening all around us, we find true peace to our soul – the Prince of Peace Who will be our covering.

He brought me to the banqueting house, and his banner over me was love. My beloved spoke, and said to me: "Rise up, my love, my fair one, and come away [Song of Solomon 2:4, 1] AMEN!

Chapter 3

Yours Is The Kingdom – Nothing Can Stand Against It

In this encounter, I was left astounded and in holy awe of our fearsome and fearless great, Conquering King! It forever changed how I see His Kingdom and His Light, and just how true it is that nothing can stand against it – no evil, no darkness, it must flee!

May you hear the Good Shepherd's voice calling you closer to His bosom – calling you to become love and light. Calling you to push back the darkness that wants to destroy you, your family, and the eternal plans that He has for you!

I returned late Saturday night from several days of travel and ministering. After unpacking, and passing physical and mental exhaustion hours ago, I could not sleep. My physical body was done, my mind was done, but my spirit was more alive than ever and won over as I was being pulled into a place of worship around 2 A.M. I stayed in that place until about 4:30 A.M. when I finally I went to bed. I remember waking at 7:30 A.M. too tired to get up, and slept until 9:30 A.M.

After brushing my teeth, washing my face and making a cup of tea, I was anxious to be with the Lover of my soul and headed for the prayer room. As I sat before Him, my whole body felt so drained, yet I was longing to go for a walk as it had been days since our last walk. After some time in prayer, I just had to go for a prayer walk and felt the Lord's pleasure in this. He knew I was so weak in so many ways and how our walks refresh me, especially when I feel so drained.

I wanted to be with just Him – not even necessarily to pray with Him, but to just be with Him, to be in His company – to have a good family chat, or the long comfortable pauses that come in a relationship that has matured, where you just enjoy each other's company without having to say anything.

With those thoughts, I left the prayer room and got ready to leave. I had many ministry admin needs pulling at me. I thought maybe I should review one of the meeting messages that I had just completed while walking, or I should keep praying as we have so much to pray for as a ministry.

As I was contemplating all of this, what quickened my spirit was to abandon both those plans and to just worship Him! To worship Him to the one song, *What a Beautiful Name*, He had given me several days ago. So, I grabbed my iPhone with my worship music playlists and earbuds, and a little before 11:00 A.M., I headed out the door. I was so looking forward to this time of just being with our Beloved Yeshua in song!

It was a beautiful late morning, the sun was breaking through the clouds, and the wind was refreshing, not too cold. I was marveling at His creation all around me – it is always a beautiful sight to my eyes and spirit. I told the Lord, *"I think we should go on the walk that takes us to the high place."* It's about a two-hour walk that passes the farmlands, up the hills to open land which is surrounded by mountains and hills, with a view of the valley and sea below.

As I was worshipping my spirit became more and more alive – wanting passionately to worship Him and proclaim His greatness, His glory, His Kingdom to anyone around me! Yet at the same time, everything within me wanted to bow before His glory – He was overwhelming my senses, and it only made me want to worship Him more fervently! I soon forgot my fatigue, for every part of my being was awakened to His glorious presence.

Soon into our walk, I became very aware of the Lord's tangible presence, as He was walking alongside on my right. I only wanted to tell Him how much I loved Him, adored Him – how He is worth everything! He then spoke some words to me that melted my heart and I started to cry. At the same time, I could not stop worshipping Him!

As I did, I could clearly perceive in my spirit, the Lord and I were not alone. His holy angels were on our left and right and slightly behind us. I felt the glory and majesty of the Lord like I have experienced on one other occasion. What it feels like to walk alongside the Lord of lords and King of kings, and at the same time the Lover of our soul – how high and noble His heart is and how His Majesty commands for all of creation to worship Him. It caused me to fervently worship Him even more.

As we continued our walk, and as I worshipped, His presence increased to the point He was now letting me see something I had never seen before. It is hard to describe in human words, but He was increasing His Kingdom all around me and letting me see just how glorious and powerful it is to the measure I was able to behold it in that moment. Even though my natural eyes could see fields, trees, roads to my right and left, my spiritual eyes were opened, and I could see His holy array gathering around us.

At first, what I could see was the increase of His holy array around my immediate surroundings. It was glorious and astounding – I was speechless and in awe! The more I worshipped, especially when I sang the chorus of that song,

> *You have no rival, You have no equal,*
> *Now and forever God You reign,*
> *Yours is the Kingdom, Yours is the glory,*
> *Yours is the Name above all names,*
> *What a powerful Name it is,*
> *What a powerful Name it is,*
> *The Name of Jesus Christ my King,*
> *What a powerful Name it is,*
> *Nothing can stand against it,*
> *What a powerful Name it is, the Name of Jesus.*[1]

He kept increasing His Kingdom around me – more and more of His holy array gathered.

---

[1] *Lyrics from song, "What a Beautiful Name," by Hillsong Worship*

Every time I sang, He kept increasing to the point when we reached the high place – the open land – before me, behind me, the valley and sea below was completely covered with His holy array – His angels! I was quickly becoming more undone yet unable to stop worshipping Him! As I looked all around me – 360 degrees – as far as my eyes could see it was all His glorious Kingdom, and at the center of it all was the Lord Yeshua!

As we walked, the manifestation of His beautiful, glorious, majestic presence – His Light and glory went before us. As He moved, it not only moved with Him, but His power and Light increased! He was allowing me to stand right next to Him in the center of it all! How can one describe the beauty of His holiness and the awe of His power?

What He wanted me to see was just how powerful His Name and His Kingdom is – how nothing can stand against it! Darkness cannot even get close – His Light literally pushes it back. I could now understand the very words He had put in my heart to sing so many days ago on a Kingdom level – *Yours is the Kingdom, Yours is the glory, what a powerful Name it is – nothing can stand against it!*

This position in Him – this protection, is for all who will follow Him wholeheartedly. For all who will pay any price to be one with Him. For those who will deny themselves, take up their cross and follow the Lamb wherever He may lead, who will not love their own life unto death. For those who will be found without spot or wrinkle. That this is the glorious position His Bride will have in Him to accomplish His will in the dark days ahead.

What also came to mind in this moment, was the scripture He had put into my heart a couple of months ago to meditate on daily, "*I pray that you may be filled with the knowledge of His will, with all wisdom and spiritual understanding, that you may walk worthy of the Lord, fully pleasing Him, being fruitful in every good work, increasing in the knowledge of God. Strengthened with all might, according to His glorious power, for all patience and longsuffering with joy* [Colossians 1:9-11].

He was letting me see and feel how His glorious power strengthens us with all might, and how those who are for us are far greater than those who are against us. We all know the scripture, right? I can assure you this day it took on a whole new meaning to me enlarging my spirit! I stood in awe, gazing all around me, undone, and thanking Him for allowing me to have this experience with Him. It will forever change how I see the battles that we as believers are called to not only walk through, but are expected to overcome by being love and Light.

I could only shout as loud as I could, for all to hear, just how worthy He is! How He is worth everything – any price one may need to pay to be found to walk worthy of Him – to be able to be positioned in that place of glory in Him where nothing can stand against the eternal kingdom plans He has for us. To be able to crown Him with the honor that belongs to Him alone.

Beloved, we are in a serious spiritual battle against darkness that wants to stop His Light from coming forth in our lives. That wants to stop His Kingdom from being formed within us, in our loved ones, in our families and in our cities and nations. That darkness wants to stop us from fulfilling our high and lofty destiny that each of has in Him.

If you are facing dark times, battles within and without, be encouraged and assured that those who are for us are far greater than those who are against us. Now is the time to surrender all and let His refiner's fire come and do the purifying work within your soul that the darkness within can be replaced with His love and Light.

I promise you, if you are willing to let go of the things that are hindering the plans your Good Shepherd and the Lover of your soul has for you, you will not regret it!

Be assured though, it will cost you everything, but you will find there is no price too high to pay to be the Bride of Messiah – positioned in Him, in His glory to rule and reign with our Great King Yeshua for all of eternity!

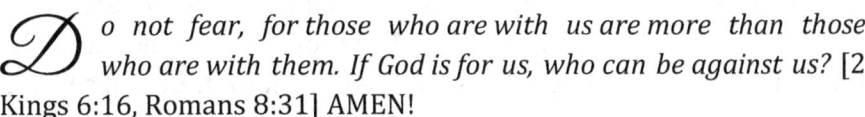

*D*o not fear, for those who are with us are more than those who are with them. If God is for us, who can be against us? [2 Kings 6:16, Romans 8:31] AMEN!

Chapter 4

There Is No Fear In Love

For how great is His goodness and how great is His beauty, and how unfathomable is His passionate love towards us. In this encounter, I was undone by not only His love towards us, but what He experiences when we love Him with an undivided heart.

May you hear the Good Shepherd's voice calling you closer to His bosom – calling you out of fear and into His perfect love. Calling you to that place of abiding in love, where your gaze will meet the heat of His gaze, drawing you deeper into His heart.

*I*t was another beautiful spring morning walking the hills of Kerry with the Lover of my soul. I was deep in thought and prayer as I approached a familiar sheep pen that was on my right. It was one that I had passed many times before. As I got closer, I noticed the sheep were at ease – meaning they were not startled by my approach and did not move away. Some were lying down; others were grazing near the fence that separated us by just a few feet.

I stopped for a moment to greet them with my usual greeting, *"Kisses right between the eyeballs and hugs forever to each and every one of you seen and unseen."* As I stood there, enjoying their beauty, glancing around their field I observed that some seemed quite comfortable lying against a large rock, others were content to graze either by themselves or in groups of two or three. Some faced the road that I was on, while others had their back to it. But all seemed content and at peace, not bothered by me in the least, even though I was quite close to them.

One ewe, in particular, caught my attention and I would speak loving, kind words of affection to her. The more I spoke, the more her gaze became fixed on me as she stood across from me. After a few moments, some of the other sheep stopped what they were doing and were now staring at me.

They amused me – I had not encountered this before. So, I told them all how beautiful and special they were and how much the Lord loved them for He created them. I marveled at the beauty of each one and how uniquely different He had made them, so different, yet still from the same flock.

I continued to stand there speaking loving words to them. The more I spoke, the more intently they seemed to gaze at me. Soon, even the sheep that were quite comfortable lying down, and the ones that had their backs to me were now gazing at me. I marveled and could not understand what was going on! They had now surely gotten my attention – taking my heart hostage!

I did not want to leave them. Everywhere I looked I saw these beautiful eyes gazing into mine, watching my every move – making me feel like I was the most exciting and important being on earth, which I knew I was surely not! I could have cried! I felt so loved and honored by them. Their undivided attention made me feel so special. And, it was not feeding time, nor did I have anything to offer them but love!

I cannot explain in words what was being released into the atmosphere all around me in these given moments. I know that may sound crazy to some – how can sheep in a field make someone feel loved, honored and so special? But that was what was being released tangibly into the atmosphere around me and what my heart was absorbing. I was overwhelmed by what I was feeling and could not stop the tears that were quickly welling up in my eyes.

It caused me to cry out to them all saying, *"I feel so loved and honored by you. You make me feel so special."* I stood there looking at each and every one of them – my eyes meeting their gaze. There was nothing in me that wanted to leave them. They had melted my heart and I just wanted to stay with them forever, giving them hugs and kisses! How could I tear myself away from them? My heart was torn to leave but time could delay no more and we had to part ways.

It was hard to turn away and continue on without them – nothing in me wanted to. It was in that moment that the Good Shepherd started speaking to me. Making me aware He was there with me, allowing my heart to feel His ever so noble heart of love that He has towards His own.

There is no fear in love. He is the Good Shepherd – His perfect love casts out all fear. When His sheep have matured in love, they do not fear Him, they are not afraid to let Him get close, no matter how intimate it may feel. In that place of love that is matured, our gaze meets His – gaze for gaze. We are no longer afraid to gaze upon the Lover of our soul no matter how inadequate, broken, or weak we may feel. We no longer run from Him, or try to keep a comfortable distance between us.

Instead, we do not fear His gaze upon us – His scrutiny into every detail of our lives, correcting and perfecting those things that concern Him and us, no matter how painful it can seem to us at times. That perfect love causes us to run to Him even faster with our gaze solely upon Him, His every word – His every move, even more intently. For we learn to trust in His ability to prevent us from stumbling, to present us blameless before the presence of His glory in triumph joy.

When our gaze is solely upon the Good Shepherd, where He has our undivided attention – meaning no other lovers but Him, we need to know it stops our Bridegroom King right in His tracks! Our undivided heart gets His attention and melts His heart. It makes Him feel so loved, honored and special as He alone deserves. When in that place, there is nothing that can cause His heart to move away from us. Instead, we get to feel how deep His love is and the joy our relationship brings Him,

In that position of love – that place of intimacy, when our eyes meet His gaze, it captivates His high and lofty, noble heart bringing Him great joy! Causing Him to want to shower us with His love and affection, reassuring us of the peace and security that can only be found in an intimate relationship with Him.

We feel His fiery, burning, jealous love calling us deeper into His eternal plans and purposes. We feel the Good Shepherd's heart not wanting to move on without us! He sees our end. He says it is good, very good, if we will let Him take our ashes and make beauty out of them.

When we face seasons of heartache and afflictions, if we stay in that position of love, becoming perfected in love – being conformed to His character in our words, thoughts and deeds – no matter what our eyes see or our flesh may feel, we will feel the heat of His gaze leading and guiding us in the way we are to go. He will gird us with strength and make our way perfect.

Beloved if that is you – feeling pressed, shaken in ways that are making you feel uncomfortable, suffering losses that seem unbearable, be of good cheer and know that the Lover of your soul is fighting for you! No one cares more about your destiny being fulfilled than our Great King.

Keep your gaze upon Him. Abide in love. And be encouraged, in that place of suffering, a transformation is taking place. For our suffering was always meant to transform us until Christ is completely conformed within us. Why? So He can qualify us to be the Overcomer – the Bride of Messiah.

And to His Bride, He will be faithful to provide every access, provision, and protection that she needs to navigate the dark days that are only getting darker. She will be filled with His glory and clothed with His Light pushing back the darkness, so that His Kingdom can come and His will be done in the nations.

The Bride of Messiah maturing in love is the Lord's answer for the difficult days that are coming. Those who will rule and reign with Him over all of creation for all of eternity.

There is no fear in love; but perfect love casts out fear, because fear involves torment. But he who fears has not been made perfect in love. And you will seek Me and find Me, when you search for Me with all your heart [1 John 4:18, Jeremiah 29:13]. AMEN!

Chapter 5

He Gently Leads Those Who Have Young

I had only been in Kerry a few short weeks when this encounter took place. I was still getting familiar with my rural surroundings – and the wandering sheep that I often encountered while out walking the land in prayer. I had not ever been amongst the sheep as I find myself so often these days, and I was trying to understand them – their character and temperament, and why they end up outside their sheepfold.

It was becoming a daily adventure – walking the land praying while running into sheep outside their sheepfold. I noticed those outside their fencing do not wander too far from their fold. Instead, they stay close wanting to get back in, but seem to not know how.

So, I found myself not only praying much for Ireland on these walks, but now for the sheep to find their way back to the safety of their sheepfold! This prayer walk was no different. Yet, as I began this walk, I had no idea that the Master Teacher had divinely orchestrated events in such a way to teach me a very powerful lesson in leadership, all preparing me for a painful trial that I was going to walk through in a short few months.

May you hear the Good Shepherd's voice calling you closer to His bosom – calling you back to first love. Back to obedience, for our obedience was always meant to restore us back to an intimate, love relationship with the Father and the Son.

I had decided to go to the high place that I had recently discovered that overlooks the valley and sea below. I quickly headed out the door, thankful that the weather was pleasant for late October – it was overcast, but no rain and mild for this time of year. Every now and then the sun would peek through the gray clouds, as I walked the quiet roads praying.

When I got to that place – I stood there feeling the Lord's heart. Soon an utterance of prayer came forth for Ireland, this isle known as the Emerald Isle that He loves without measure, for her to fulfill her destiny as a nation. For her to know the heights, lengths, depths, and breadths of that love – to save, heal and restore her back to her rightful inheritance that can only be found in Him, as a people, tribe, tongue and nation.

The morning was now turning into early afternoon, so I began my way back. As I continued praying in the spirit, I decided to take the long way back. It is a narrow, winding road, up and down hills, that passes many farmlands before bringing me to the main road. Often on this road I would encounter a wandering sheep or two. We somehow managed to get by each other, without them being too frightened, for there was not much room to pass by, as comfortably as they would have liked!

I was soon on this road, and as I climbed the first of two hills, I was starting to feel fatigued. It had been a couple of hours since I started walking, and honestly, I just wanted to get back to the house – I was not feeling too spiritual at all. But I kept praying in the spirit, despite my weak flesh, encouraging myself that I only had another half-hour to go.

With these thoughts, I really hoped I would not encounter a wandering sheep. As it could take some time before we could pass each other, for I did not want them to run too far away from their sheepfold. So, at this point, in my tiredness, I was just not in the mood for a delay.

When I came to the top of the hill, seeing the road below to the next hill, I was not too happy to see two ewes at the bottom. They were across from a farmhouse where the road begins to climb uphill, bringing you out to the main road. This part of the road is particularly narrow, so I was wondering how to pass without causing them to run up the hill onto the main road. I was concerned, if that happened, a car could hit them, which I could not bear for that to happen.

So, with these thoughts in mind, I made my way down the hill, praying – praying for the Lord to send His angels to help us get by each other. My prayers were not being answered, and the very thing I feared they were now doing – running up the hill towards the main road! I stopped at the bottom of the road across from the farmhouse – trying to woo them back, speaking, *"Peace be still"* and kind words to them, to no avail.

I kept praying, greatly concerned, as I could not see them anymore for the road curved. I asked the Lord to send His angels ahead to stop them and cause them to turn around and come back. I waited, standing in that place for I knew if I continued it would cause them to run further in the wrong direction onto the main road, possibly being injured or killed.

After a few moments, I saw their heads appear in the distance walking in my direction. As soon as they saw me though they stopped, not wanting to take another step forward. So, I turned around walking back up the hill I had just come down, hoping that would give them a comfortable distance between us to get back to their sheepfold. It seemed to work. As I glanced behind me, they were now walking down the hill.

Once they got to that place across from the farmhouse they stopped. It was the widest part of the road, so there was a chance we could get by each other. I started walking towards them, and they turned around and started walking up the hill again. This time they did not run, but walked a few yards and stopped. I was able to get to the farmhouse while they stood looking at me. They clearly wanted to come back, but were afraid to get too close to me so they could pass by.

We were at a standoff! I kept praying to no avail. I was tired, starting to get frustrated and just wanted to get back to the house – this walk was turning out to be longer than I had planned. I considered going back the way I had come, but it would be even longer, so I decided against that thought.

As I stood there, contemplating what to do, a thought came to mind to hide myself behind the half-wall that was at the end of the farmhouse's driveway. It was off the road a few feet and angled just enough that if I crouched really low, I would be out of their sight, and just maybe the sheep would walk by, and we could both go on our merry way!

By now I had nothing to lose, except more time, so I did exactly that. I waited a few minutes and nothing – no sheep in sight. I was going to stick my head out to see if I could see where they were and decided not to. I waited a few more minutes. It felt like forever. If anyone saw me, they had to seriously wonder what in the world I was up to – talk about odd behavior!

My weary mind could take no more. I had to stick my head out to see where they were – wondering if I was just wasting time sitting there. Right in that moment, right before I did, the two ewes walked right by me – victory! Hallelujah! I jumped up and praised the Lord, thanking Him for making a way. Thanking Him for showing me what to do and keeping the sheep safe! For I was truly relieved no harm came to them. And, I was truly relieved I could be on my way – no more delay.

As I walked up the hill, I kept thanking the Lord for rescuing them and me. And, what seemed like such a foolish idea, to hide myself behind that wall until they passed, was really all Him, His infinite wisdom. I kept thinking about if I had insisted, in my weariness, frustration or insensitivity, to go up the hill, because I was anxious to get back, how I could have hurt the sheep. Best case they may have been injured. Worst case they might have been killed. I was so thankful the Lord had given me great grace to wait, to be patient, even though nothing in my weak flesh wanted to.

Later that evening, I was contemplating all of this before the Lord one more time – thanking Him, marveling at His wisdom. He then spoke about what I had experienced, and what the Good Shepherd had wanted me to learn. I just wept and wept, asking the Lord, *"Please help me to never forget this priceless lesson. Please help me to not ever be careless or reckless with Your sheep's hearts. Please forgive me Lord for any way that I have in the past."*

So often His sheep find themselves outside His sheepfold – outside that place of truth, purity, holiness, peace and security that can only be found in Him. They know where they belong, but for whatever reasons they wander outside of His pen. Those reasons can be many; wounds not healed, fear, confusion, unforgiveness, religion, false doctrines, deception, pride, rebellion, rejection, neglect by leadership to feed them – there are many, many reasons. So they wander away from Him.

At the same time, His sheep have a longing to return to where they belong. So many do not wander too far – but try to stay close to their fold. Often though they cannot find their way back on their own, as quickly as when someone helps them – for a blindness has come over them. It is easy to find a way out of His pen, but most times it is harder to find the way back in, once on the outside of it.

When those who know the way back into His sheepfold, first come in contact with those that have found themselves on the outside, it can frighten them. At first, they can run – trying to get away as fast as they can. Why? Because those people look and sound so foreign to them, making them feel uncomfortable in their ways that are not the Good Shepherd's ways. So, at first, they run trying to get away.

But they run only so far before turning around wanting to return to where they belong. If those who are to help lead them back are patient, share truth in love and extend them much grace, the sheep will no longer run in the opposite direction.

Instead, they start the journey of coming back into His fold. They will come at the pace that is set before them by those who were sent to lead them back. Those leading are to lead gently those that are young – spiritually immature until they can digest the meat that has been given to them. Some will come more quickly than others.

The Lord further told me that if had I insisted on going at 'my pace' in walking up that hill to the main road, by disregarding what might happen to the sheep, I would have the potential to not only injure them, but possibly kill them. So too is it with His sheep. Meaning, if I insist in leading at my level of maturity, what I think they can handle, it could injure or destroy them, spiritually speaking. It could stop them from fulfilling their destiny.

These were frightening words for me to hear – but words I needed to hear, for I would not ever want to be careless with a single heart. No doubt I have in my walk over the years, but the Lord knows it would not have been to intentionally hurt someone. This surely had me see, what may sound like common sense to most, in a whole new light – His Light. Seeing the Good Shepherd's heart towards His beloved ones and how His patience will win many back to Him.

At the same time, there are times to deposit truths, seeds, into these precious lambs' souls that are outside His sheepfold. He will divinely arrange for those times to take place in one's life. They may be hard truths for some to hear.

Some may become startled, offended, even rejecting those truths. For a season they may want nothing more to do with you as a leader, as a pastor, as a mother or father – as a friend, and run quickly away.

But it does not mean we are to withhold feeding them the spiritual food that will nourish them – no matter how hard it may sound, or however uncomfortable it may make one feel. At the same time, it is so important it is done in His timing. That we are ever so sensitive to His leadership and wisdom in how to do so. It requires great grace, patience, long-suffering, humility and loving-kindness, especially when your flesh wants to do the exact opposite.

After that deposit takes place – those seeds that have been sown, there can be a season where we are no longer actively involved in someone's life. The Good Shepherd, at times, will remove from their life those who were sent to help them find their way back, if they are not responding. Why? Because they need time to digest what has been sown. If they are given more when they have not embraced, digested, what has already been given, it could push them further away from Him.

As well as, they have been given just enough truth – spiritual food. To awaken them out of their complacency so they can find their way back, if they desire.

Additionally, those seeds need time to grow and mature,

enabling them to come back at His pace – not ours. Meaning, we do not force them back prematurely by putting our timing, expectations, or judgments on them.

He is the Good Shepherd. He knows what each of us need, and no two situations are identical. He is the way, the truth and the life. He will always lead us in the way that brings us to truth, no matter how hard it may seem to hear at times. For it is truth that sets us free. It is truth that brings us back to the narrow road that brings eternal life.

In His faithfulness, He will be faithful to bring those into our lives who will teach and lead us in the way we are to go. Even if it seems frightening to us initially – for His ways are not ours, nor His thoughts our own. And, at the same time, He will provide every grace, strength and courage that we need to follow the Good Shepherd wherever He may lead. For His sheep will know and obey His voice – doing so from that position of abiding in love.

Ultimately, our Beloved King wants to restore us back to an intimate, love relationship that can only be found in Him. He doesn't want any of us outside His sheepfold. But it requires a response – our obedience. Our obedience was always meant to restore us back to intimacy – keeping us in the intimate confines and safety of His sheepfold.

The Bride of Messiah will be a bride of intimacy. She will know and follow the Good Shepherd's voice. She will know her Bridegroom King intimately. She will be one who lives solely to satisfy His every desire – not her will being done, but only His for all of eternity!

He tends His flock like a Shepherd: He gathers the lambs in his arms and carries them close to his heart; he gently leads those that have young [Isaiah 40:11, NIV]. AMEN!

CHAPTER 6

KEEP ASKING, KEEP SEEKING – KEEP KNOCKING

It can be easy to lose hope and become discouraged in this lost fallen world. Even more so, if we have lost our way in our walk with the Lord, finding ourselves paralyzed and bound up in fear, or other obstacles in our lives that are stopping us from moving forward in His plans for us. In this encounter, I experienced just how relentless His jealous love is to rescue and free us, and especially where man has failed to help us.

May you hear the Good Shepherd's voice calling you closer to His bosom – calling you to keep asking, keep seeking, keep knocking, for in due season you shall reap a reward!

After spending most of the day somewhat discouraged trying to find my way in how to go about the plans the Lord has for me, I asked, *"Do you think we can just go for a walk Lord and pray?"* It was still Shabbat and the sun was going to soon be setting. So I hurried out the door a little after 3:00 P.M. The sun was still shining, and the cold winter air was refreshing to my soul. It was good to get out and have this time with the Lord that was becoming more and more frequent.

There is something special about the sun shining on a cold winter day in Kerry. The rays of light seem to highlight the beauty of the mountains, hills, pastures and coastal land, causing them to glisten even more beautifully. As I walked, I was enjoying His creation, thankful for this time to be with the Lord, feeling His comforting presence all around me.

After about 30-minutes or so, I found myself on one of the windy, quiet back roads that is surrounded by farmland. The sun was going down quickly, and I was thinking I should be able to make it back before it got dark. With those thoughts in mind, I soon came upon a ewe, on my right, with her head sticking out of the wire fencing facing the road.

When I got to where she was, I stopped to greet her, as she stood there, eating the grass that was on the other side of her field. I spoke what was becoming my typical greeting to all the sheep or lambs, *"We love you and bless you, kisses right between the eyeballs to each and every one of you, and hugs forever."* I further told her, *"The grass is not greener on the other side – it's exactly the same. You need to eat the grass that is in your fields."*

Where she stood was a wooded area that had open pastures in the distance. There was a big farmhouse nearby, and I was pretty sure she belonged to whoever owned that house. At this time, though, I did not know that she was actually stuck. I was still learning much about the sheep, that were becoming my nearest companions, and I did not understand them too well, yet.

So, I continued up the hill on my way, thinking that however she got her head through that wire, surely she will be able to get it back through when she is done eating the grass on the other side. When I got back to the house, I did not give it any more thought.

The next morning, after my time of prayer, I asked the Lord, *"Do You want to go for another prayer walk?"* So once again I headed out the door, this time a little after 9:15 A.M. It was a quiet Sunday morning and I was feeling the stillness all around me, as we walked and prayed. For some reason, I decided to go the same way I went the afternoon before, which normally I don't do too often – go the same way back to back.

I soon approached that place where I had last left the ewe from the day before. And to my horror, I could see that she was still standing in the exact same place, with her head sticking out of the wire fencing! My heart sank! I felt horrible for her, knowing that she had been standing in that place since 4:00 P.M. the day before, and probably even longer, and no one had helped get her free.

I felt even worse that I had left her the day before not realising she was stuck. My heart was grieved that she stood there all night long, not able to move. And, I could have helped her if I had paid more attention to her needs.

I told her how sorry I am that I had left her – how I did not know that she needed help! How sorry I was that she had to suffer like this with no one to help her – stuck in that place all night long. I was thankful that it did not rain during the night, as she would not have been able to find shelter. I told her that I would help her.

This was all new to me. I had not ever gotten this close to the sheep before. I did not know what to do. I had helped many back into their folds, by patiently helping them find a way back in, but this was different. I asked the Lord to help me – to show me what to do. As I got near, she became frightened and pulled forcefully backwards. Her horns were stuck in the wire above, and the closer I got, the harder she pulled. I kept praying and speaking to her kindly, reassuring her that I was there to help her, not hurt her.

After a few minutes I stopped, as her frightened eyes met mine. I did not want her frightened, nor did I want her to hurt herself from pulling back so hard. I was concerned if I tried to do anymore, I would cause her harm. The wire seemed so tight around her throat, and I thought that she could possibly slit her throat if she pulled too hard – which I would not ever forgive myself if something like that happened.

I kept praying, asking the Lord to help – asking Him to send someone who knows what to do. As I looked around the only viable solution seemed to be the farmhouse that was nearby. I told the ewe, *"I am going to go get help – I promise you, this time I will not leave you until you are free. I will be back."*

So I ran to the farmhouse that I was pretty sure she belonged to. At first, I was a bit hesitant to knock on the door, as the house was pretty quiet like its occupants might still be in bed. I thought of the ewe stuck below, and lost all fear of offending and knocked really loud and waited. No answer. I knocked even louder. I waited some more. No answer. I knocked one more time, to no avail.

I was not sure what to do now. This was a very quiet road with few houses. I went back to the ewe, more determined than ever to help get her free. I prayed some more asking, *"Lord, where are the shepherds? Please send me someone that will know what to do."*

Right in that moment, I turned around and saw a man with a small boy in the distance up the hill. My heart was so thankful. I quickly ran to them, explaining the situation, asking if he would help. Once we got back to the ewe, he took a step towards her, putting his hand on her head, and as he did, she pulled back so hard that she somehow got free from the wire!

I felt so foolish, and told him I did not know what to do. That if only I had done that, I would not have had to bother him. I asked him, *"If she could pull her head out, why didn't she until now?"* He did not really know why, but shared that even when the sheep get caught in the bramble, they will not free themselves without help. That it is like they become paralyzed – like a self-defense mechanism kicks in, even though in reality they are actually exposing themselves to more harm.

We soon parted ways, with me thanking him for helping and for all that I learned, as he had taught me so much. As I continued our walk, I was pondering all of this with the Lord. First, so thankful that He rescued that pitiable ewe – that she was now free – no longer stuck. And for how sorry I was that I did not recognise her need for help the day before.

I kept thinking about how horrible it must have been for her to be stuck like that for almost 24-hours, while others passed by, ignoring the silent cries for help. I said, *"Lord, no one wants to be stuck – nobody! It is one of the worst feelings in the world to be stuck and no way out. Nobody wants to be stuck Lord, no one!"*

It was then that the Good Shepherd made me aware of His ever so noble heart towards His sheep. The lengths that He will go to set us free from whatever is entangling us – especially when there is no one else who can or will help us. He is constantly watching over us. He cares about our every need – from the smallest to the greatest. Nothing escapes His notice.

Even though, at times, it feels like we have been forgotten, passed over, ignored by man. Our Good Shepherd will never forget or forsake us – He is fighting for us to live and not die. He is fighting for us to be restored back to the safety of His sheep pen.

Be assured the Good Shepherd will answer our silent cries of help. And just like when I knocked on that farmhouse door three separate times, to no answer. Even though that owner did not answer the call for help – that ewe's freedom was not solely dependent upon whether or not they responded. So, too, the Lord will be faithful – relentless and passionate, until He finds someone who will answer the call to help His stuck sheep become free.

Beloved, if you are one who finds yourself 'stuck' whatever it may be – anger, depression, addictions, grief, fiery trials that feel like they are more than you can bear, not knowing how to go on. Keep asking for the Good Shepherd to help you. Keep seeking. Keep knocking. He will be faithful to send the help you need – so that you can be free. No longer paralyzed by oppression, fears, doubts, failures, shame or rejection.

Instead, free to be all that He created you to be. Free to follow the Good Shepherd wherever He may lead. Free to fulfill the high and lofty destiny that He has just for you – to be the Bride of Messiah.

So I say to you, Ask and keep on asking and it shall be given you; seek and keep on seeking and you shall find; knock and keep on knocking and the door shall be opened to you. For everyone who asks and keeps on asking receives; and he who seeks and keeps on seeking finds; and to him who knocks and keeps on knocking, the door shall be opened [Luke 11:9-10, AMP]. AMEN!

Chapter 7

His Ways Are Not Our Ways

When this parable took place, it was about seven months after my arrival in Ireland. As I recall the details, it could not be more relevant for us today, as the darkness increases all around, with His eyes searching to and fro upon the nations, looking for vessels whom He can fill with His glory – His answer for the dark days ahead of us!

May you hear the Good Shepherd's voice calling you closer to His bosom – calling you out of your old ways of doing things, and into the new ways He has just for you!

It was a beautiful early April morning – cold, but with the sun breaking forth from behind the clouds often enough to warm your heart. It was the time of year when the spring lambs had been birthed. Many fields were dotted with these precious young ones, that were learning to walk on solid ground as they adjusted to the cold, wet elements, no longer protected and sheltered in the warmth of their mother's wombs.

As I headed out the door to walk and pray with the Lover of my soul, my heart was heavy. I had just walked through some challenging circumstances, and feeling like a foreigner in a foreign land more than ever. I thought of the lambs and it cheered my heart and said, *"Lord, will we go that way – the road that brings us by their field, and see how they are doing?"* I loved the lambs and just the thought to see them quickly brought joy to my heart! I had not experienced being around them before, and they melted my heart every time. I could stand there and watch them forever!

Lost in prayer, we soon came upon the field that I was looking forward to getting to. Now, this field was small and right next to the road, but the road was fairly quiet. So, when we got there, all the ewes and the lambs were laying down, resting. I marveled at their beauty and how peaceful and comfortable they seemed in that place of rest.

Within moments of being there, though, a small boy caught my attention. He was about eight years of age, and the house he lived in was directly across from this particular field. He was eating a banana, rather nonchalantly, as he crossed the road to go into the sheepfold. This boy now had my curiosity wondering what he was going to do in the sheepfold? I soon found out, and it was not to my initial liking!

While eating his banana, he walked up to one of the ewes. He did not rush at her, but the opposite, there was a gentleness and calmness in his approach. He did not get too close but just close enough to disturb her, causing her to jump to her feet, along with her lambs. He then stood there for a few moments in front of them – why I did not know, but he was not in a hurry to leave them after he had unsettled them. He then quietly and calmly walked over to another ewe with her lambs, causing the same result – they jumped to their feet, not feeling comfortable to lie down or stay in the same place anymore.

After repeating this several times, I got very anxious with the Lord and cried out, *"Lord, stop him – please! What is he doing? He is disturbing them. They were all so happy and comfortable, and he is wrecking it all – they need their rest!"* So after this boy had successfully 'stirred' them all up from their comfortable place of rest, while he observed them, I could see the Lord did not want him to stop.

Instead, in that moment, I could now see the Good Shepherd's heart towards His flock! My heart was bursting inside with what the Lord was allowing me to feel – His heart, His ways towards those He loves and who belong to Him, and they are surely not our ways!

And, before I could even think about it – without realising what I was doing, I shouted as loud as I could to this boy, *"You are a good shepherd!"* He turned around from where he was standing in the middle of that field, and looked at me and just smiled - it brought such joy to my heart. I then told him, *"They really like you!"* And he just smiled even more! I thought to myself, he may be just a small boy Lord, but I believe he is one of Your true shepherds.

So too, beloved, is our Good Shepherd's heart towards us. In His love, goodness, and eternal plans that He has for us, He allows the storms, the uncomfortable circumstances to come our way to awaken us out of our complacency. To awaken us out of what has become too comfortable or familiar to us. To awaken us out of our old ways of doing things – those automatic reactions we have that have become a set way, making us feel comfortable, when He wants to do something new in our lives, in our relationships, in our meetings, in our churches and ministries.

The reality is if we stay in those places that have become comfortable, we will become stagnant and miss the golden opportunities to exchange our will for His. We will miss the new thing God wants to do in our lives. It is a time of new beginnings, but if we can't let go of our old ways, we will miss the eternal plans the Lord has purposed for us to walk in and will not complete the works our Father has sent us to complete on this earth.

And just like it was with that little boy, those sheep would have preferred he had not walked amongst them and disturbed their place of comfort. That would have surely made their lives easier, more comfortable and a lot more predictable. But our Good Shepherd knows what we need to prevent us from becoming stagnant.

So, in His faithfulness, He brings circumstances into our lives that will 'jolt' us out of our ways into His ways, if we are willing. If we can recognise the Good Shepherd, Who is in our midst, and not miss Him because of our preconceived ideas of what we think He is supposed to look and sound like in our lives, in our meetings and in our services.

If we are willing to let Him make His ways our ways and His thoughts our own, we can be assured in that place – no matter how unsettling or how painful it may feel, that the Good Shepherd stands ever so near, caring for every detail of our lives with the greatest of love.

And, at the same time, we need to know He is not in a hurry and will not rush off leaving us to wither up and die, but will stay ever so close making sure we are able to stand in the new place He has prepared for us, providing every grace and provision we need to do so.

Beloved, be assured no one cares more about your soul being saved – meaning the renewal of your mind until Christ is completely formed within you, and your destiny being fulfilled than the Lord.

As hard or as uncomfortable as it may be in the difficult places you are walking through, may the cry of our hearts be in this hour like never before, *"Not my ways Lord anymore, but make Your ways my ways and Your thoughts my thoughts. Lord fill me with the knowledge of Your will in all wisdom and spiritual understanding, that I may walk worthy of You, fully pleasing You, being fruitful in every good work, letting go of anyone or anything that hinders the plans You have for me, that I would no longer care what man thinks or says about me, but to live to please the only One that matters."*

If you are pursuing an intimate love relationship with the Lover of your soul – our Bridegroom King, a relationship that is encompassed in truth, purity, holiness, and intimacy – pursuing a relationship where you are no longer willing to walk in the compromise and mixture anymore, no matter what it might cost you. A relationship where you no longer want your old ways of doing things and feeling like you fit in less than ever these days.

Then be of good cheer beloved and know the Good Shepherd is fighting for you and not against you! Know that the new thing His is calling you to and is sending in your midst is not to frighten or destroy you, but bring you into the fullness of your inheritance that can only be found in Him – doing it His way.

It is easy for us to stay in a place that is comfortable. If we do though, we will have settled for so much less than what our Good Shepherd – our Great King had planned for us. Which is to be the Bride of Messiah, to rule and reign with Him over all of creation, forever! So, in the shakings that come, do not lose heart, do not grow weary and faint not – until Christ is completely formed within you, for in due season you shall reap a great reward!

For My thoughts are not your thoughts, nor are your ways My ways, says the Lord. For as the heavens are higher than the earth, so are My ways higher than your ways, and My thoughts than your thoughts [Isaiah 55:8-9]. AMEN!

Chapter 8

His Patience Wins Many

As I write these words, I vividly remember this time that took place in May 2017. I remember how hard I tried to rescue this lamb, how frustrated I became in that process, and eventually how emotional and physical weariness won over and I abandoned the mission that 'seemed' impossible to accomplish.

May you hear the Good Shepherd's voice calling you closer to His bosom, never doubting His patience will win many in these last days!

After returning from town and putting away the groceries, I was anxious to go for a walk and just be with the Lord. The weather was on par for a late May day – on the warm side, and a little overcast. I headed out the door, with a route in mind – one of my favorites that overlooks the sea and valley below, with the thought that I would be back in an hour and a half.

As we came to the place where I would stop and enjoy the view with the Lover of my soul, I could see on the road ahead that descended into the valley below, there was a lamb outside its sheepfold. She was lying down next to the fencing, and next to what I assumed was her mom on the other side. When she saw me, she initially jumped to her feet, wanting to move away, but not really sure which way to go.

She wanted back in with her flock but did not know the way, or how to do it. So with no other option, she had laid there on the outside next to her nearest and dearest, until I had come along and startled her.

My heart quickly became troubled, wanting her back with her mom and in the safety of her fields. Both ewe and lamb were distressed by their separation from each other, and if there was any way that we could help them, we would surely do so! So, in that moment, I set my heart and mind to not leave her until she was back with her mom, where she belonged.

Now, this particular area is fairly barren with open fields for miles on my right and left, with no houses in sight. The road is very narrow and traveled mainly by the locals, so you would not run into a car too often.

As I got closer to the lamb, trying to figure out how to get her on the other side of that fence, I was praying and asking the Lord to help me in every way possible. In her fear of me, the unknown and what she was not used to, she had now run down the road that leads into the valley below.

I stopped in my tracks, calling out to her, *"Peace be still, the Lord loves you"* and other words of loving-kindness to reassure her we were there to help her, not harm her. I asked the Lord to send His angels ahead to help her turn around and come back.

After about ten minutes, she started walking back up the road to where her mom was. In that time, I was able to find an opening under the fencing large enough for her to fit through and only inches from where her mom was now standing. That was probably how she got out to begin with – mommy ewe you are so smart, thank you for showing me! I became quite hopeful! If we could just get her in front of that opening, how easy it would be for her to be back where she belonged.

I patiently waited for her to make it back to that spot. It took some time, a lot of love and gentle coaxing, with me getting on her level – on my knees so that my height would not intimidate and frighten her. And at the same time, I was far enough away from that opening that she could find it on her own, yet near enough to help her not to miss it.

It took a lot of prayers asking the Lord to help her – to not be frightened but to keep taking one step forward, to not go backwards. Asking Him to help her see that opening clearly and to give her whatever she needs to walk through it.

Patience seems to have worked, and she was now standing right in front of that opening – Praise the Lord! I was thrilled and thought this precious lamb would soon be in her fold, and I would be on my way back to the house. I did not know this was only the beginning of many attempts to help her through that opening.

As I stood low before her, encouraging her to walk through it, she just stood there baaing. She seemed paralyzed and blinded to that opening. I honestly was baffled in how she could not see it – it was so obvious! And at the same time, I desperately wanted her to go through it. I asked the angels of the Lord to help her – guide her and direct her, that she would be able to go through.

To my discontent, she walked away and then started running, baaing as she went, in the opposite direction. Her mom became more distressed following her on the other side of the fence, baaing. As I watched, waiting and hoping she would turn around and come back, it became clear this was not going to happen.

As she went further away from her flock, I went after her, praying, *"Lord help! Help her to turn around and come back."* While I was still far from her, I could see a car coming towards us.

In one way this was good for it caused the lamb to turn around running back in the right direction, for she chose to run right in front of the car. At the same time, though, this caused me to soon lose sight of the lamb altogether, for when the car slowly passed by that precious lamb was now being herded down the road into the valley below, by the car!

I no longer heard any baaing, and I feared we had lost the lamb for good, but I had not given up hope. I walked back to the place where the road descends below. I could not see the lamb anywhere.

My heart was more grieved than ever for this little one to be returned to her fields, if possible. So, I started walking down the hill to see if I could find her. I was soon overjoyed to see her in the near distance walking back up the hill! I quickly turned around, optimistic that we could still get her to go through that opening, as she was once again heading that way.

I waited at the top of the road for her, near that opening. As she made her way closer, I encouraged her with peaceful, loving-kind words. She was not as fearful as before and walked calmly by me. I did not get too close, wanting her to stay calm and not miss that opening.

As she approached the spot, she stood right in front of it. After hesitating for a few moments, seeming blinded to the safety that opening would provide, she continued walking up the road. This time, in the opposite way of the valley below, baaing as she went, looking for another way into her fields.

By now much time had gone by, and I was becoming tired, thirsty and weary. This prayer walk was becoming a lot longer than I had planned. Which would be fine, if we could get the lamb back in her fields, but that prospect seemed to be fading.

As I walked in the direction of the lamb, an idea came to mind restoring hope and strength to keep trying! There was a metal gate that was a part of her fields that was near the direction she was headed. If I could open it and get her to head towards it, the mission would be accomplished. And would be so much easier than what I had been trying.

While evaluating this option, a new concern presented itself. With some effort, I was able to open the gate, but it swung wide open. In order for me to herd this lamb through the gate, I would have to leave it unattended. Because of the other sheep in this field, although not near the gate, I did not want any of them to escape – that would surely not be helpful to anyone!

As I was pondering this over with the Lord, the car that came by earlier was headed towards me. I wondered if maybe this man might be willing to help by standing guard at the gate, while I herd the lamb into it?

With that thought, I stopped the man and asked if he would be willing to help? He was not interested replying, *"No, you know how farmers are with their land"* and drove off. Thinking to myself that no, I did not know how farmers were – I did not know what he was talking about!

I felt more weary, frustrated and helpless than ever. I was pretty sure we could get the lamb into her fields this way, but I was not willing to do so at the cost of potentially hurting the other sheep, by them possibly escaping because there was no one to guard the gate. Feeling discouraged, I abandoned this idea but knew it was the right thing to do.

So, the only option was for her to go through that opening. The lamb was now in front of me, halfway between the gate and that opening under the fence, distressed and baaing. Still determined to not leave her until she was safely with her mom, I walked towards her, gently herding her towards that opening, not getting too close, but close enough to guide her.

As we got near that opening, I was praying for her to move towards it, for angels to guide her through it. All to no avail! This time, she ran back down the road that leads into the valley below, baaing all the way!

So, after more than two hours of trying to restore her back to her fold, I stood there defeated and discouraged, and just cried. I was in tears for I did not want to leave her that way, but at this point, I felt I had no option. My heart hurt for her. I wanted her back with her mom, back in the safety of her fold. Instead, I last saw her running the wrong way, distressed, baaing, crying for help until she was no longer in sight. I was in tears because no matter how hard I tried, I could not help her.

Heartbroken, I said Lord, *"It breaks my heart to leave her, but I just can't do anymore."* The Lord soon started speaking to me as He knew my thoughts. I was now thinking about His sheep – not the sheep of the fields. I was thinking about a particular beautiful, young, precious lamb, that we loved greatly, that had been put into my life to disciple. I had been trying to help her overcome some of her fears, all to no avail, so it seemed.

As much as I tried to reach out, in patience, in loving-kindness, trying to be a spiritual mom, she resisted me in every way possible. It had become painfully clear that it was up to her to either embrace me or not. How I could do no more, but to hold her in a position of love in my heart, and to pray for her.

Thinking about all of this, I said, *"Lord, what are You saying to me? Is this her end – in her fears, stubbornness, pride and rebellion will she not make it back into Your fold? Will she not make it because she has refused Your endless love – Your rescuing help, causing her to become blind to the way that will bring restoration and peace to her soul? Oh Lord if this is so, this is not good!"* I cried even more! I no longer cared about how late the hour was, how tired, thirsty and hungry I had become.

My heart was consumed with this precious young woman that I desperately wanted to help. My heart was torn in pieces not wanting to leave this lamb that I had been trying to get back into her fold, for the Good Shepherd was letting me feel His noble, beautiful heart, His love and the lengths He will go to rescue us, in a measure that my heart was able to bear.

As I stood there sobbing, feeling I had no other option but to leave this lamb for I was not able to help her, the Lord kept letting me feel His sorrow. That as painful as it is for Him, at times, He has to let go, or what 'seems' like He is letting go. Not because He wants to, but because He will not go against our free will.

He will not force us into His eternal plans, but will give us more opportunities than we deserve to willingly return back to that place of intimate fellowship with Him so we can complete the works our Father has for us to do. And, if we are willing, He will provide more than we need to do so.

As this impacted my spirit, I bawled even more. It was more than my weary mind and emotions could bare in that moment – to think this precious, little one, that I was now thinking about, might not fulfill her destiny to be the Bride of Messiah.

There is only one way that restores us back to that place of intimate fellowship with our Bridegroom King – it is to deny ourselves, take up our cross and follow the Lamb wherever He may lead.

Many today, like that lamb who came to that opening, are hesitating, blinded by fear causing them to not enter, but instead are running the opposite way. If we are not willing to yield to the Good Shepherd's voice when He calls, by exchanging our will for His, we will miss fulfilling His eternal plans for us – to be the Bride of Messiah.

Many today in the Body of Messiah, like that precious lamb, are refusing His help for many different reasons; fear, wounds, shame, doctrines of demons, pride, stubbornness, rebellion – there are many, many reasons.

Often in our Christian walk, in our weariness and frustration, we try to find another way to accomplish a goal that looks more logical and easier, but can lead us and others into danger if we are doing something that the Good Shepherd is not asking us to do. Or, if we cross a boundary that is not ours to cross by forcing our will on others.

That if we do, we will end up not only harming ourselves but those the Lord has put in our lives to influence. Just like when I had opened the gate to get the lamb into her fields. If I had gone ahead with that plan, I would have not only been disobedient because I did not have the farmer's permission to open his gate, although it was a good intention, but in that place of disobedience I would have the potential to harm the other sheep, by exposing them to the dangers outside of their fold.

The Lord is jealous over us. He does not want any of His sheep to perish, or suffer unnecessarily, by those who try to come in some other way. He is the Good Shepherd. He is the Door that leads to eternal life. Those who belong to Him must come in the same way they went out. Anyone who comes into His sheepfold any other way is a thief and a robber.

As I began my journey back, my heart was heavy thinking upon these things. I was thinking of both the natural lamb I had to leave behind, hearing her baaing in the distance. And, the spiritual lessons the Master Teacher was teaching me about His lambs that 'seem' to be going the wrong way.

As I did, the Good Shepherd shared His heart one more time saying, *"Just because you cannot see the lamb right now, it does not mean she will not find her way back to that opening. It does not mean she will not be restored back to Me. It just means for now you are not able to see when or how that might take place."*

When this encounter happened over two years ago, I went

through a season – a little over a year, where I did not have any contact with this beautiful, young lamb that ran away from me. But during that time, the Lord did a wonderful work in her heart – restoring her to her rightful identity to be the Bride of Messiah.

He brought restoration to our relationship without me doing anything after the Lord said no more, other than praying for her and staying in a position of love towards her, believing He is able to draw her back, in His timing.

He is the Master Builder and faithful to those who have a 'yes' in their hearts. Meaning, they may not be where they need to be yet, but they belong to Him and have a 'yes' to surrender to do it His way. Therefore, He will be faithful to restore them back into His eternal plans, and doing so with great care and joy!

Beloved, if this is you or you know others that 'seem' lost or wandering, be encouraged that if we are faithful to keep praying, to keep extending patient love to the unlovable, staying humble – low before them, and keep believing the Good Shepherd is able to draw them back into His fold, we too will see the fruit of that patient love multiple in our lives.

So often when we think it is the end of something, the reality is the opposite. It is the beginning and continuation of His eternal plans working in our lives – as challenging, sorrowful, or how off-track it may seem at the time.

But His patience will win many in these last days. Our job as believers, as leaders, is to be 100% yielded vessels, exchanging our will for His, being patient in battle, so He can manifest His eternal plans in and through us that the Father and the Son may be glorified.

Being patient in love, patient in battle is more times than not painful and lonely, with many opportunities to be rejected, as we are often misunderstood or falsely accused. But, if we are to be the Bride of Messiah, we need to know we will suffer greatly for others to come into their rightful inheritance that can only be found in our Great Redeeming King.

Our sufferings are the sacrificial love of the Lamb flowing in and through us, conforming us until Christ is completely formed within us. That is the call that is upon all of our lives – to deny ourselves, take up our cross, and follow the Lamb.

It is the call for His Warrior Bride to overcome by the Blood of the Lamb, by the word of her testimony, not loving her own life unto death, until and until every captive that can be set free is free – until every soul that can be saved is saved!

The Lord does not delay and is not tardy or slow about what He promises, according to some people's conception of slowness, but He is long-suffering (extraordinarily patient) toward you, not desiring that any should perish, but that all should turn to repentance. But let patience have its perfect work, that you may be perfect and complete, lacking nothing [2 Peter 3:9, AMP; James 1:4]. AMEN!

Chapter 9

Blinded By Pain

Sometimes in life, we can become blinded by pain, or circumstances that seem too much to bear. In this encounter, I experienced the never-failing love of the Good Shepherd to rescue His own to the uttermost, bringing freedom.

May you hear the Good Shepherd's voice calling you closer to His bosom – calling you out of captivity and into the fullness of the freedom that He has for you!

After my morning time of prayer with the Lord and taking care of a few things for the ministry, I was looking forward to getting out for a walk with the Lord. The weather wasn't the best, nor was it the worst for a cold, wet winter morning. The showers had stopped, but there was still a threat of their return as the sky above was dark and overcast.

I decided to go on our route that winds in between the quiet farmlands, that eventually brings you onto the main road that takes you into town. It was winter time, so the roads were quieter than usual. While lost in my thoughts and prayers with the Lord, after about a half-hour, I made my way up the hill that brings you onto the main road. Although it was cold, I liked the fresh air that was blowing on my face, refreshing me, as I continued to pray in the spirit.

As I approached the bend, I heard baaing in the distance. It caught my attention for I could discern it was coming from one who was distressed and in trouble. It was open land on both my right and left, with a few farmhouses in between. The fields on my right, were rocky and steep, being part of a mountainside. The fields on my left were scattered, full of bramble bushes and gorse that led to a small creek below with fields on the other side of it.

The cry for help was coming from the fields that were on my left, but I could not see any lamb or ewe in sight. I stopped to search the fields intently with my eyes. As I did, every now and then a weak, pitiable baa would fill the air. This caused me to look even harder, asking the Lord to help me, *"Where is it Lord?"* I soon spotted it in the distance, very near the creek.

From afar, this did not appear to be too difficult of a rescue mission, and I quickly found a way over the fencing and made my way down the fields, to the ewe that had somehow gotten herself entangled. She was caught in a bramble bush and had become entangled in its' thorny branches.

As I got nearer, I could see she was in quite a mess! There were several thorny, bramble branches woven into her long, wool coat – all around her head, neck, horns, and legs, so she was not able to move. Every time she tried to move, the thorns dug into her coat and skin, keeping her a prisoner to them. She was weak and my guess, by the state of the soil around her, is she had been there for at least a few days. There was no way for her to free herself without someone's help.

I stood near, speaking kindly, reassuring her I was there to help get her free. Although not too sure how to do so, without the bramble's thorns tearing me to pieces. They are sharp and merciless, and I did not want to be injured by them. If only I had a pair of heavy gloves to protect my hands.

Thinking Lord, *"How do we do this?"* He soon reminded me of a heavy plastic bag in my pocket. It is what I used for the cow's treats, and I had meant to take it out before I left, but forgot about it. I was so glad I had not done so, as I could use this to protect one of my hands – Praise the Lord!

With a plan of protection in place, I quietly approached the ewe. She was frightened by me, and at the same time, not able to move much, so that worked, initially, in both of our favors in getting her free. I started with the branches that had entangled her legs.

As I did, she cooperated nicely by not moving. So, one by one, I was able to pull them out of her thick coat, causing her to regain freedom to her legs. We were making slow, but good progress!

Trying to get the thorn branches that were tightly woven around her neck and horns, proved to be much more difficult. Because of the way she was positioned and entangled in the thorn bush, I could not get a hold of the branches. She had struggled a lot trying to get herself free before I had gotten there, so these were particularly hard to pull off. They were like a noose pulled tightly around her throat, buried deeply in her long, wool coat.

Seeking the Lord for His constant help and wisdom, knowing that I had surely never done this before, our only option was to reposition the ewe, so I could access her head area. At least her legs were free, so that was now possible. I moved to the other side and was able to turn her around 180 degrees, so her head was no longer stuck in the thorn bush, enabling me to work on removing those branches.

All of a sudden, she panicked, and with great force turned around, 180 degrees, and forced herself right back into the thorn bush, with me in tow! Because the bush was next to the creek, and the ground not level, as she turned around, I grabbed ahold of the bush so not to fall into the creek – ouch!

I was baffled – why did she do that? She went head first right back into the very thing that was hurting her and holding her captive – causing her more pain and distress! The thorn branches were now even tighter around her horns, head and neck. It seems like we took two steps forward, only to take ten steps backwards!

I kept praying for the Lord's help. *"Help her Lord to not be so frightened. Help her to know that she was headed the right way – the way that will set her free from this bondage and pain. That her captivity may have become familiar to her, but it is hurting her, not helping her."* As I prayed, I tried again to turn her around. As I did, I was able to quickly get the branch off her neck – that was a miracle!

As I tried to loose the one that was woven tightly around her head and horns, she started to become anxious. I steadied her, with my arms and body, while still pulling at that last branch. It seemed impossible to get loose! I kept tugging at it and holding her at the same time. In the blink of an eye, the release came, and the ewe was free – Praise the Lord!

Another miracle for there was nothing in the natural that could have caused that branch to give way. I could only give great praise and thanks to our Good Shepherd, Who is the only One Who can set the captives free!

She stood there for a second until she realised that she was free. She then ran across the field baaing, to join her fold in the field across from the creek. As I walked across the fields making my way back to the road, I stopped for a moment to watch her. As I did, she too stopped and turned my way, and we just looked at each other – her gaze meeting mine.

I was so happy she was finally free. I could feel the Good Shepherd's heart once again, thanking Him for this time and for allowing me to feel His high and noble heart towards His sheep. I was feeling the joy in His heart when we are free.

We all go through times in our walk, where we become blinded by pain. By situations that seem hopeless – situations where we have suffered much loss. Where our prayers seem to have gone unanswered year after year, causing us to embrace the lies the enemy whispers into our minds about ourselves, about others – our situations. Causing us to lose sight of the Good Shepherd's plans for us by becoming bound up in pain, sorrows, despair, defeat and discouragement.

Beloved, if that is you, be of good cheer. Not only does our Good Shepherd, the Lover of our soul, love you – He cares for your every need! You may feel trapped and paralyzed right now, taking two steps forward to find you have gone several steps backwards – just like that ewe.

And no matter how hard you try to fight the good fight of faith, by fasting and praying – by surrendering your will for His, for breakthrough and deliverance to come, you feel more helpless than ever with no help in sight.

You may feel your prayers have become weaker and weaker – somedays just a whisper, crying out for help. Barely holding on to the thread of hope you have left, that against all odds, your breakthrough will come.

Sometimes when our pain – or fears have become a familiar place, when the help comes, we run in the opposite direction. Head first right back into the very things that have been hurting us and our relationship with the Lord. Wrong attitudes, offenses, unforgiveness, addictions. When we do, we take others with us, causing pain and sorrow to those relationships. We become blinded by our pain. Feeling forgotten and forsaken, for our trials seem too much to bear.

But be assured the Good Shepherd knows how to rescue when nothing we do in the natural can. He does not want you to lose heart, nor to grow weary or to faint. Instead, He is reminding you today, that in due season you shall reap a great reward.

That just like that ewe, even though her baas were becoming weaker every day, yet in that place of captivity, she kept crying out. And because she did, her Rescuer came and set her free! Her deliverance came in a split second, giving her victory over the very thing that was trying to overcome her, restoring her back to freedom!

Yeshua, our beautiful Savior – our great eternal High Priest, Who forever liveth to make intercessions for us, was pierced, scourged, bruised and afflicted that we might live and not die. That we would live in the freedom of the fullness of His truth that sets our captive souls free. Free from all fear. Free from all bondage. Free from all hopelessness and despair.

Free from every way this world's ways of doing things has stained our souls with its filth and compromise. Free from every way our emotions have been taken captive by the lies the enemy tries to force upon us and our loved ones.

Free from all religion and fear of man so that we can be in an intimate love relationship with our Bridegroom King. Free to live so we can surrender all to Him, that we can become all that we were created to be – the Bride of Messiah. When we overcome – victory brings freedom.

And *the Lord, He is the One who goes before you. He will be with you, He will not leave you nor forsake you; do not fear nor be dismayed. But now since you have been set free from sin and have become the slaves of God, you have your present reward in holiness and its end is eternal life. For you, brethren, were [indeed] called to freedom; only [do not let your] freedom be an incentive to your flesh and an opportunity or excuse [for selfishness], but through love you should serve one another* [Deuteronomy 31:8, Romans 6:22, AMP; Galatians 5:13, AMP]. AMEN!

Chapter 10

Resurrection Life

Life is often not what it seems. And, if we are in a hurry, we can often miss His redemptive plans for us. In this encounter, I experienced the faithful, steadfast love of the Good Shepherd to resuscitate what appeared to be dead, back to life.

May you hear the Good Shepherd's voice calling you closer to His bosom – calling you out of despair, discouragement and defeat into resurrection life!

*I*t was a cold, wet, windy, winter day. Yet, despite the elements, I refused to let them be a deterrent from walking the land with the only One Who can save, heal and restore us back to our rightful identity that can only be found in Him – the Lover of our soul! With that thought in mind, I wrapped myself up and headed out the door.

The roads were quieter than usual, as I walked and prayed on one of our familiar routes. As we made our way over and down many hills, with farm fields around us, and the mountains in the near distance, one thing was surely obvious. With all the recent rains over the past weeks, the land was saturated not able to absorb much more. Therefore, it was overflowing, with many new springs bursting forth in places that would normally be dry.

As I came onto the main road – about halfway in our walk, I was pleasantly surprised that I was not completely drenched. Even my shoes, for the most part, were still dry, for which I was thankful to not have cold, wet feet. That is not a pleasant feeling and one I like to avoid, if possible! Thank you, Lord, for every way You have me covered.

With a heart of praise and thanksgiving, I soon approached the part of the road that curves around. Giving you the choice to either keep going into town or to turn onto the coast road, that brings you into the quiet, nearby townland of Ardea. As I approached the curve, I saw a small pick-up truck parked on the side of the road, near a gate that belongs to a field of sheep.

I was wondering what was going on? Not only because it is an awkward part of the road to stop on, but in all our walks I had not ever seen anyone stopped near this gate. And, in general, I had rarely seen the owners with their sheep. Which that in itself troubled my heart on many occasions, as I had observed so many hurt, wounded, limping, lame, sometimes bleeding sheep and lambs.

Always causing me to ask the same questions, *"Lord, where are the shepherds? Why are they not taking care of these little ones that need help? Why don't we ever see them – where are they?"* So, this vehicle surely got my attention.

As I got nearer to the gate, I was surprised to see a man, on his knees, covered in mud trying to free a ewe from the feeding trough where she had gotten entangled. I stood and watched, and as I did my heart quickly sank. It appeared the ewe was dead, for she was lying lifeless in the mud and muck, all around her.

On closer observation, I could see she had gotten her horns caught in the metal openings at the bottom of the trough. I thought the farmer was trying to remove her body. For that I was thankful – that her nearest and dearest would not have to suffer emotionally, by seeing one of their own lying dead, any longer than they had to.

My heart was sad, yet at the same time, thankful that this man arrived when he did. I was thinking how in all these months of walking the land, being so close with the sheep, we had never seen a farmer helping his sheep in trouble. And we have seen many in trouble, day after day, with no one coming to help them. Even though it appeared to be too little too late in this case, at least he was here amongst the sheep.

As I watched, it was not an easy task to get this ewe free. He worked fervently trying to do so. At one point, I thought I saw her body move. I started to get hopeful. *"Is she alive, Lord? Or, did her body move, because of his hard labor to free her?"* My gaze was fully fixed on this situation more than ever. After a few more moments, it was true! She was alive and not dead, after all! Hallelujah! She was now thrashing around violently trying to free herself. This made this man's job even harder!

I desperately wanted to help him. And for a split second, in my selfishness, I thought of my clean clothes and dry feet. I thought if I helped, I would be covered in mud and muck, and so much for my comfy, dry feet! I counted the cost, and there was no question, she was worth any discomforts I might endure!

I quickly shouted to this man, who had no idea he had an audience of one this whole time, *"Do you need any help – can I help?"* He turned around, surprised to see someone. And just in that moment, the ewe was free, jumping to her feet! She was startled for a second, before running to join the rest of her fold.

I said to the farmer, *"Thank God you came – you were here at the right time. I thought she was dead!"* He was kind, humble and very gracious telling me how he was just driving by, and that these sheep are not even his own. That he saw she was in trouble, not sure himself if she was alive or not. I thanked him again, even more so, considering this ewe did not belong to him, yet because he took the time to stop, her life was saved.

As we parted ways, I could feel the Good Shepherd's heart encouraging me. That after more than a year of not ever seeing a shepherd tending to the sheep who were neglected and in desperate need. That even though this is a serious prophetic warning in our land to the leadership, at large, and how they are not taking care of His sheep – sometimes leaving them for dead. That in His faithfulness to us as a people, tribe, tongue and nation He is bringing forth the good shepherds.

It is a new season for Ireland – time for the true pastors and leadership to come forth to be seen and heard! This man, who rescued the ewe, represents that true leadership, and what it is going to look and sound like in many ways – nameless, faceless, selfless.

The Church, at large, in all nations, is full of pastors and leaders who care only for their selfish gain, their reputation and building their own kingdoms, with it often being done so at the expense of the sheep.

For most do not want to soil their outer garments or disrupt their comfortable ways of doing things to intervene in the broken, messy lives of those in desperate need of a Redeemer. Those precious ones who are in need of being resurrected, from the muck and the mire that surrounds them.

That despite that sad fact beloved, the Lord wants us to be encouraged. He is raising up, in this hour like never before, those who will come forth and take care of His flock – not just the fold they have been given to steward.

They will not necessarily have the credentials that man demands of them, but will have the Good Shepherd's heart burning within. That will qualify them by heaven standards for they will only be about the Father's business.

They will be the nobodies by man's standards, but highly esteemed in heaven. They will know that the sheep do not belong to them but to the Lord. And will treat them as such by not being lords over them, trying to control them. Instead, they will give the lambs and sheep freedom to come and to go into the sheepfold as needed, by encouraging them to grow and mature into the high call that is on each of their lives.

These leaders will be fearless and fearsome ones, who will live the laid down life of the Lamb – by denying themselves, taking up their cross and following the Lamb wherever He may lead. And, because of it, they will walk in true kingdom authority, which is clothed in the nature of the Lamb.

These true pastors – true leaders will arise and build the broken-down walls starting in the Church. And, starting with the lambs and sheep that desperately need His faithful, consistent, loving attention and kind care. Teaching and encouraging them to carry their own cross – to die to self, their own ambitions. Teaching them how to become vessels of noble use – ones who will be without spot or wrinkle, that they might be filled with the glory and be the Bride of Messiah.

And, despite the apostasy that is rapidly growing in the Church, opposing the true teachings of Yeshua, with doctrines of demons, these true leaders will not walk in compromise and mixture.

Equally, they will steward the sheep from a position of love, joy, peace, patience, kindness, goodness, faithfulness, humility and self-control. They will steward from a position of being nameless, faceless and selfless – not from a position of selfish gain.

They will not ignore or reject those outside their fold. Instead, they will be sacrificial with their time leading them in the way of truth – into the truth that brings life. Leading them into an intimate, love relationship with the Bridegroom King – a relationship that is clothed in truth, purity, holiness and the fear of the Lord.

And, when these true shepherds do, they will lead those who are bound up in darkness, bondage and self-inflicted captivity without any hope of being rescued, back into His marvelous light – into the freedom that can only be found in our Beautiful Savior and Redeemer.

They will lead those that have been left for dead into His resurrection life – so they can be used mightily by the Lord of the Harvest in these last days, to bring in the great harvest!

In order to do so though, we must first die to self, by surrendering our will for His in our words, thoughts, and deeds. We must become like a grain of wheat that falls into the ground and dies, so we can be filled with the same resurrection power that raised Yeshua from the dead, bringing forth much fruit.

When that transaction takes place, be assured beloved, that many springs of living water are going to burst forth in the most unlikely places that were once dry, bringing forth resurrection life, all to His glory!

This is the Good Shepherd's heart for us; for our families, for our communities, villages, cities and nations. May it be done unto us according to His Word, and to the level of our faith to those who believe!

Most assuredly, I say to you, unless a grain of wheat falls into the ground and dies, it remains alone; but if it dies, it produces much grain. Though the cords of the wicked have enclosed and ensnared me, I have not forgotten Your law. Behold, I long for Your precepts, In Your righteousness give me renewed life. I am Yours, therefore save me; for I have sought (inquired of and for) Your precepts and required them [as my urgent need] [John 12:24, Psalm 119:61, 40, 94 AMP]. AMEN!

About The Author

Ever since the return to the love of her life, the Lord Yeshua, in 1999, Tracy Hogan has walked closely and intimately with the One whom her soul loveth and adores. In 2007 she had a life-changing experience where the Lord allowed her to witness some end-times events. In 2009 the Lord came and awakened her in a different way, by revealing His high and holy standards of what it means to be pure in His eyes, and just how pure one's heart has to be if they are to see His face. It jolted her to the core. It was the beginning of her journey to become His bride.

Tracy's call is to the nations. To prophetically teach the Word of God to help prepare the Bride of Messiah for the Lord Yeshua's soon coming return. For her to know how to dress herself in her wedding garments – to be a Bride who has made herself ready – one who will be without spot or wrinkle, and one who will be ready for her wedding day. This bridal preparation comes by teaching her truth, purity, holiness, and in helping nurture in her an intimate love relationship with our Bridegroom King, through worship, intercession, and warfare.

Tracy resides in Ireland, where she founded The Voice of My Beloved – A Call to the Nations Ministry.

The Voice of My Beloved
A Call to the Nations Ministry

www.thevoiceofmybeloved.com

About Manifest Publications

Manifest Publications is the publishing division of Manifest International, LLC. Our objective is to help like-minded ministries and writers produce and distribute materials which proclaim the Gospel of Jesus Christ to all the world and equip the global Church for unity and maturity.

www.manifestinternational.com
www.manifestbookstore.com

www.ingramcontent.com/pod-product-compliance
Lightning Source LLC
Chambersburg PA
CBHW052206110526
44591CB00012B/2099